WESTCHESTER PUBLIC LIB

7   9100 381 990 5

W9-AQH-329

DISCARDED

BIG
babies

little BABIES

DK Publishing

DK

LONDON, NEW YORK,
MELBOURNE, MUNICH, and DELHI

Written and edited by Lorrie Mack and Penny Smith
Designers Clemence Monot, Gabriela Rosecka, Sadie Thomas
Consultant Kim Dennis-Bryan, Ph.D., FZS
US Editor Margaret Parrish
Publishing Manager Bridget Giles
Art Director Martin Wilson
Category Publisher Mary Ling
Production Controller Claire Pearson
Production Editor Siu Chan
Jacket Designer Pamela Shiels

First published in the United States
in 2010 by DK Publishing
375 Hudson Street, New York, New York 10014

Copyright © 2010 Dorling Kindersley Limited

10 11 12 13 14 10 9 8 7 6 5 4 3 2 1
177162—02/10

All rights reserved under International and Pan-American Copyright Conventions. No part
of this publication may be reproduced, stored in a retrieval system, or transmitted in
any form or by any means, electronic, mechanical, photocopying, recording, or
otherwise, without the prior written permission of the copyright owner.
Published in Great Britain by Dorling Kindersley Limited.

A catalog record record for this book
is available from the Library of Congress.

ISBN 978-0-7566-6165-6

Color reproduction by Alta Images
Printed and bound by
Star Standard, Singapore

Discover more at
www.dk.com

Come with us
and meet all
kinds of adorable
baby animals.

what's inside

bright baby

Adult silver leaf monkeys are gray, but the babies are bright orange! We're not sure why—it may make it easy for their moms to find them, or it may let other monkeys know there are new arrivals in the group.

Here I am with Mom. She feeds me milk (and so do other mothers in our troop). When I'm older, I'll eat young leaves and fruit.

These monkeys live in troops with one male leader and between 10 and 50 females and babies. All the females help to look after the babies.

All change!

It takes three to five months for a baby to turn gray. The head, hands, and feet are the first to fade. When a monkey is about four years old, it's ready to have babies of its own.

The troop spends most of its time up in the trees. When it starts to get dark, the monkeys settle down to sleep—all in the same tree. All the babies cuddle up to a female at bedtime.

happy family

Albatrosses find a mate, then stay together for life. Mom lays just one egg—she and Dad take turns sitting on it. When it hatches, they both look after the chick. After a few months, it can fly by itself.

Most albatrosses nest together in large groups called colonies. All these nests look the same—they're high mounds made from grass, mud, seaweed, and poop.

Albatrosses spend their lives flying thousands of miles over the sea, or floating on the waves. When it's time to mate and raise their chicks, they go back to the same rocky island where they were born.

These birds love to eat fish and seafood. Sometimes they follow boats and bring back scraps that have been thrown overboard. Both parents fly off looking for food and only return to their baby to feed it.

safe ride

A Nile crocodile mom makes her nest deep in the ground near a river. She lays about 50 eggs there, then guards them well to make sure they're safe.

Crocodile babies, called hatchlings, are about 12 in (30 cm) long. They stay with their mom for up to two years.

When my babies hatch, they make a chirruping sound so I know I have to dig them out. Then I carry them to the water.

Get me out!
Croc eggshells are tough. When a hatchling has trouble breaking through, Mom cracks the egg by rolling it between her tongue and the roof of her mouth.

speedy spots

Cheetahs are the speediest land animals on Earth—they can run as fast as cars on a highway! They have spots like leopards, but they're much smaller, with longer tails. Cheetah babies are called kittens.

Cheetah kittens love play fighting. When they're a few months old, Mom will take them with her so they can learn how to hunt for real.

My mom usually has three to five kittens at a time—she looks after us until we're about a year old, then we go off on our own.

Can you see me?

When a kitten is born, it has long fur on its back that helps it to hide in tall grass. The fur starts to disappear when the kitten is about three months old, and it's gone by the time the baby is two.

Cheetah moms have to protect their babies from hungry lions and hyenas. But once the kittens are about five months old, they can run faster than all their enemies!

moose on the loose

Moose (sometimes called elk) live in forests near lakes and swamps. They like wet places and feed on water plants as well as grass, lichen, and tree bark.

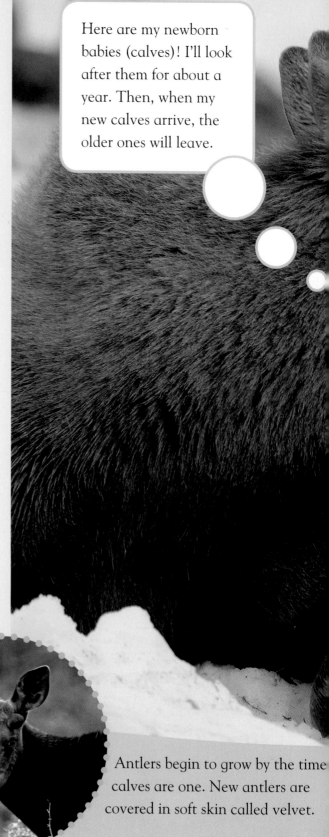

Here are my newborn babies (calves)! I'll look after them for about a year. Then, when my new calves arrive, the older ones will leave.

Antlers begin to grow by the time calves are one. New antlers are covered in soft skin called velvet.

A boy thing
Only males have antlers—they use them to fight for females. Antlers fall off in winter and grow in spring.

A calf can swim by the time it's two weeks old. Sometimes a moose goes completely under water to escape from annoying flies.

13

splish, splash

Dolphins live in water, but they breathe air like we do. Unlike us though, they have nostrils on the tops of their heads. Babies (called calves) are born under water and swim right away.

Mothers help their newborn calves to the surface to breathe.

14

Dolphins are light colored underneath and dark on top. This is good camouflage—they are hard to see against the dark water below, or the sunlight above.

Click! Click!

To find their way in murky water, dolphins make a clicking sound. They listen for the echo, then use this to work out what's nearby. This is called echolocation.

wait for me!

When a mother duck finds a safe spot near water, she makes a nest from leaves and grass, then plucks soft feathers from her chest to line it. When she's laid her eggs, she sits on them for around a month until they hatch into ducklings.

I lay up to 13 eggs. A day or so after my ducklings hatch, I lead them to water. They stay close to me all the time, so I can keep them safe, and warm at night.

Baby clothes

Ducklings are covered in down—brown on top and yellow underneath. They don't get adult feathers until they're a few weeks old. That's when they leave their mom. Baby ducks can swim and dive for food as soon as they hatch.

bathing beauties

These Japanese macaque monkeys live near pools of naturally hot water. In cold, snowy weather, they climb into the steamy bath to warm up.

Moms have one baby at a time. They feed it milk until it's nearly two years old. Babies stay with their mom, even after she has had another baby.

Come on, jump in—

Adults share the job of looking after babies. When the air is frosty, the little ones cuddle up in an adult's thick fur.

Clean behind the ears?

Macaque monkeys live together in troops of about 40 animals. They groom each other to keep clean. Grooming is also a good way for a monkey to make new friends.

When I've finished my bath, I'll have something to eat. My favorite foods are fruit, seeds, flowers, insects, and birds' eggs.

the water's great!

I'm not bald!

American bald eagles aren't really bald—their pale head feathers just make them look that way. Eagle parents make huge nests that are as wide as a man is tall. They can keep the same nest for up to 20 years.

Moms usually lay two eggs. Mom and Dad take turns sitting on the eggs until their babies (called eaglets) hatch.

I'll be gray until I'm five or six weeks old, then I start getting black feathers. But I won't get all my grown-up feathers until I reach five or six years.

At first, the mom always stays near her eaglets. Later, when they're about 20 weeks old, they can take care of themselves.

Mom and Dad deliver food—small fish, birds, mammals, and reptiles. Adults flap their big wings to hover over the nest.

it's a pup's life

Most hyenas live in large family groups called clans. The leader of a clan is usually female. Hyenas like meat—they hunt prey or eat dead animals.

Here's Mom, licking me again! She looks after me and my brother. She'll feed us milk until we're a year old, or even longer. Sometimes she brings us meat to eat.

Spotted hyenas make giggling sounds—

Home, sweet home
Hyena pups live in a small earthen burrow called a den. They are watched over by the adults in the clan.

they're known as laughing hyenas.

just hangin'

Opossums are marsupials—moms carry their babies in a tummy pouch. Babies drink milk, but adults eat anything from plants and mammals to birds, snakes, insects, and human garbage.

I have up to 13 babies—when they're born, they could all fit in a teaspoon. When they get a bit bigger, I will carry some of them on my back.

Opossums are very intelligent—

Going solo

Mom feeds her babies in the pouch for about 10 weeks. They leave her then, but return to snack for another few weeks.

Tail talent

Opossum tails grip tightly—babies can swing from tree branches, but adults are too heavy, so they use their tails for balance.

they're even smarter than dogs.

big bird

Ostriches are the world's biggest, heaviest birds. They can't fly, but they can run very fast. Ostriches live in Africa, where it's hot, but they don't have to drink— they can get water from the plants and insects they eat.

Mom and Dad show me what to eat and look after me until I'm about a year old.

An ostrich chick grows inside its egg for about 45 days.

While it's there, it calls out so its parents, who will know its sound.

Ostriches lay the biggest eggs of any

Both parents sit on the eggs until they hatch. Mom does the day shift, since her feathers are speckled and she's hard to see against dry grass. Dad's black, so he takes over at night.

The chick pecks its way out with its egg tooth—a hard piece on the end of its beak.

When the chick first hatches its dad looks after it.

bird—20 times bigger than hens' eggs.

cool cubs

Polar bears are the biggest bears in the world.
Moms sometimes have one baby (or cub),
and sometimes three, but usually there are
two. Cubs will stay with their moms until
they're two or three years old.

Underneath
their long, white fur,
polar bears have a layer
of fat called blubber.
When they get too hot,
they roll in the snow
to cool down.

Mom gives birth inside a snow den. When each baby is born, it can fit in her paw. All three stay put until the babies are about three months old.

Baby bears learn about the world by playing and exploring—just like you do!

29

pretty in pink

Most flamingos live in warm places, always near the water. Their feathers are very pink, a color that comes from the food they eat—shrimp, and tiny plants called algae.

Mom and Dad both produce a kind of milk, which I drink for around two months.

Flamingos build shallow mud nests in a colony with other flamingos. Moms usually lay just one egg, which hatches into a chick in about 30 days.

Chicks have straight beaks—after

Cold feet

Flamingos often balance on one long leg, and they even sleep like this. Experts think they do this so they don't get too cold when they stand around in water.

Chicks are gray for their first year or two. They can look after themselves after about two months.

a year or so, they start to curve.

heavy weight

Rhinoceroses are big and heavy. They're usually shy, but they can be fierce if they're frightened. A rhino doesn't see very well, so it might charge a tree, thinking it's an enemy. Rhinos are vegetarian.

Rhinos live in hot grasslands or forests. They keep cool by finding shade or standing in water.

Dust bath

Rhinos protect their thick skin by rolling in dust. This coats the skin, keeping out insects and bright sunlight.

Hello! My mom will look after me for about three years. By that time, I'll be almost as big as she is.

A rhino has just one

Rhinos have either one or two horns. Mothers use these to protect their calves from lions, tigers, and hyenas.

baby (or calf) at a time.

mini me

Sea otters are furry mammals that live in the water. They like to float on their backs in shallow seas, and they even sleep like this. Sometimes they wrap themselves in seaweed so they don't drift away.

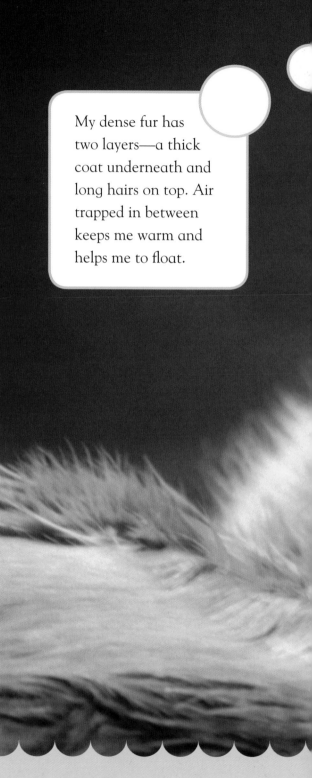

My dense fur has two layers—a thick coat underneath and long hairs on top. Air trapped in between keeps me warm and helps me to float.

Hold me, Mom
Mom gives birth to one baby, or pup, which has all its fur. Her front paws have rough pads on the inside so she gets a firm grip on things—like her pup!

Newborn pups already have teeth.

By about four months, pups can eat solid food and swim. At six months, they'll leave Mom behind.

here I come...

Tigers are the biggest cats of all. They eat meat and hunt for large prey like deer, buffalo, and wild boar. Tigers love to swim, and always live close to water.

Play and learn

From the time they're babies (when they're called cubs), tigers play at fighting and hunting. By the time they're a year old, they can kill real prey.

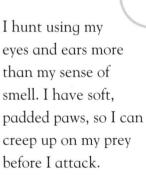

I hunt using my eyes and ears more than my sense of smell. I have soft, padded paws, so I can creep up on my prey before I attack.

Tiger moms have two to four cubs, which are born with their black stripes. She looks after them for up to two years.

Newborn cubs are blind, so their moms have to carry them. Like all cats, tiger moms carry their babies carefully in their mouths.

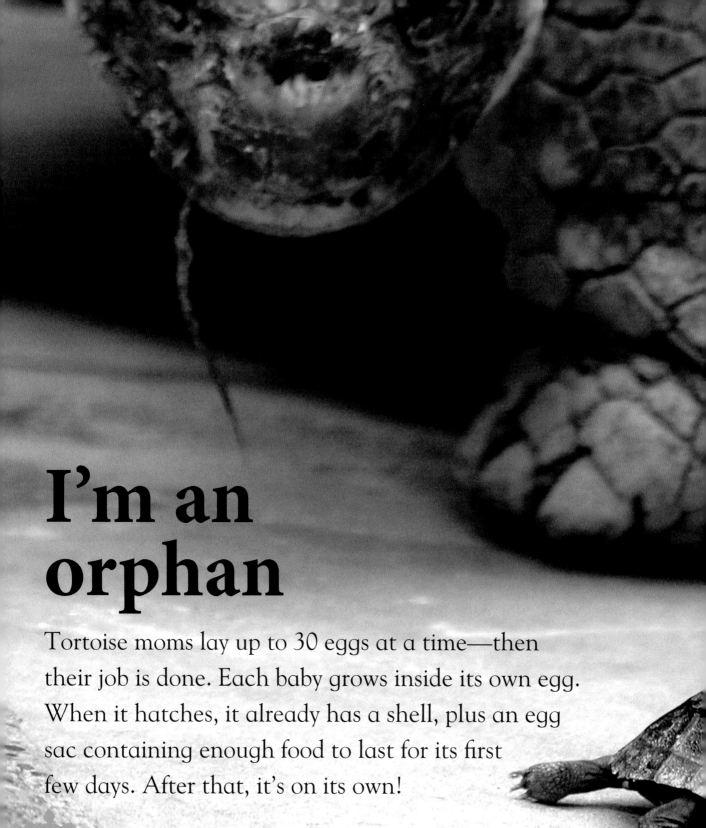

I'm an orphan

Tortoise moms lay up to 30 eggs at a time—then their job is done. Each baby grows inside its own egg. When it hatches, it already has a shell, plus an egg sac containing enough food to last for its first few days. After that, it's on its own!

This baby could have a very long life—the tortoise is one of the longest-living creatures on Earth. Some reach 150 years or more!

Hello, world

Nearly there...

I'm out!

A baby tortoise takes a few hours to break its way out of the egg. Eggs are laid in nests in the sand. The time babies take to grow inside (and whether they're male or female) varies with how hot or cold the sand is.

39

the seal deal

Seals live mostly in the sea. They glide gracefully though the water, but they're very clumsy on land. Seals belong to a group of animals called pinnipeds. This means "fin feet."

Arctic fur seals live near the South Pole. The babies—called pups—drink their mother's milk for about four months.

40 When they're born, some seal pups

When you see a performing seal with a ball on its nose, you're really looking at a California sea lion, like these. They're very smart and easy to train. When the pups are about two months old, they already know how to swim and hunt with their mothers.

I'm an elephant seal. I have only one baby at a time, so he gets all my attention.

What's my name?
Elephant seals are very big—that's one reason they got their name. Adult males are two or three times bigger than females like this mom.

are so dark, they're almost black.

family favorite

Elephants are the largest land mammals on Earth. They live in herds led by a female, and they all teach and protect the little ones.

Calves learn how to use their trunks—for grabbing food, sucking up water, or holding on to a friend.

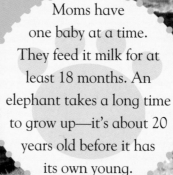

Moms have one baby at a time. They feed it milk for at least 18 months. An elephant takes a long time to grow up—it's about 20 years old before it has its own young.

Oh, good—this mud
will cool you down.
And if you get too hot
again, try flapping your
ears—that should help.

It's easy for young bears to climb trees. Adults usually stay on the ground, since their long claws make climbing difficult.

put 'em up!

When the weather gets colder, the female brown bear digs out a den in a sheltered spot—under a rock or a tree. She sleeps here through the winter, and while she's there she gives birth to up to four tiny cubs.

Cubs stay with their mom for three years or more. She teaches them to find food and learn their way around.

Male bears live alone.

They never see their cubs.

perky pigs

Once upon a time, all pigs were wild animals. Thousands of years ago, humans tamed them and now most pigs live on farms. Special pig farms are called piggeries.

Where's my supper?
Pigs have a keen sense of smell that helps them find food—this is a good thing, since they can't see very well. Pigs are clean animals, but they still like to roll in mud to keep cool.

Pig moms have between eight and 12 babies, or piglets. Sometimes they have lots more! Some pigs are pink, some are black, some are brown, and some are spotted.

Males are boars and females are sows.

Dinnertime
Piglets feed on their mom's milk for about seven weeks, then they eat anything. By the time they're three, they're all grown up.

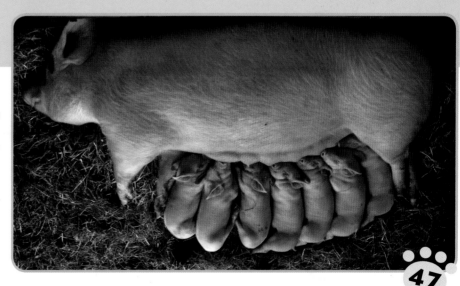

neck and neck

Giraffes are the tallest mammals in the world, because they have such long necks. Babies (called calves) can run around almost as soon as they're born, and by the time they're four, they're all grown up.

Newborn giraffes are about as tall as a grown man, and almost as heavy.

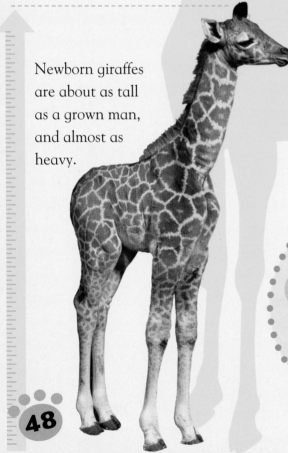

Adult giraffes have small horns covered in skin. Baby giraffes have even smaller horns. These are very soft, but they get harder as the baby grows.

Giraffe moms

While I'm a baby, Mom keeps me tucked away from the herd in a shady place. She's never far away, though, and comes back often to feed me.

take turns looking after each other's babies.

who, who?

The great gray owl is one of the
biggest owls in the world. When
it opens its wings, it's about
as wide as you are
with your arms
stretched out.

I am an owlet. Both my
parents look after me.
If a bear or wild cat
comes near, Mom and
Dad chase it away.

Just born

A mother owl lays up to five eggs at a time. She sits on them so they stay warm. When the eggs hatch, the babies (owlets) are covered in fluffy down.

Great gray owls live in forests. They don't build nests—they move into nests that other birds don't use any longer.

Young owls stay in the nest until they're about four weeks old. Sometimes they tumble onto the ground and their parents guard them there.

get moving...

Bison are sometimes called buffalo. Females live in large herds of up to 60 with their babies (called calves)—they protect them fiercely from danger. Males live alone or in small groups.

When I was first born, Mom kept me away from the rest of the herd. We all live together now, but Mom will take care of me until I'm about a year old.

Bison get rid of ticks by rubbing themselves against trees. Sometimes, if lots of animals use the same tree, the bark gets worn away completely.

What's for dinner?

Bison feed on grasses, herbs, and shrubs. In the winter, they dig in the snow with their hooves to get at plants underneath.

Bison calves are a light reddish-brown when they're babies—they don't get dark coats until they're around three months old.

Both males and females have humps on their shoulders and horns on their heads. Calves grow both at about two months.

home on the reef

Clown fish live in coral reefs among the tentacles of a sea anemone. Moms lay their eggs there—one mom can lay thousands of eggs.

I'm the dad. Mom leaves her eggs as soon as they're laid, then I guard them until they hatch into babies, called fry. This takes around 10 days.

At birth, Dad leaves his fry alone.

When they first hatch, all clown fish are male. Later on, some of them turn into females so they can lay eggs.

Taking care

While Dad guards the eggs, he fans them with his fins. This helps them to get enough oxygen and stops plants and animals from settling on them.

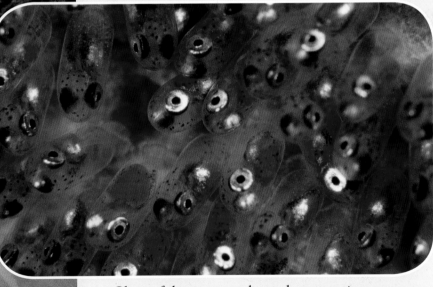

Clown fish eggs are about the same size as peas. They look like shiny orange bubbles in the sea, but they fade as the eggs develop.

They have to manage by themselves.

I can see you...

Meerkats live in groups of up to 40 that are called mobs. They build big underground burrows, where they sleep and raise their babies. At all times, sentries stand nearby and watch for danger.

My pups cry out when they're hungry. The ones that cry the loudest usually get the most food.

A meerkat mom usually has three or four babies, called pups. With help from other adults in the mob, she looks after them until they're around four months old.

A meerkat's coat keeps it warm at

The dark band of fur around a meerkat's eyes cuts glare. Unlike humans, a meerkat can look into the sun—very useful for spotting birds that want to swoop down and eat it.

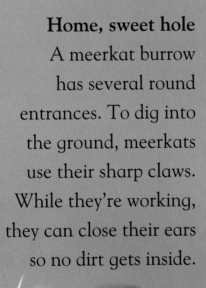

Home, sweet hole

A meerkat burrow has several round entrances. To dig into the ground, meerkats use their sharp claws. While they're working, they can close their ears so no dirt gets inside.

night, yet cool in the hot sun.

hold on tight!

Pangolins are the only mammals that have scales. Pangolin moms have one baby at a time, and they look after it for around five months. It will be a couple of years before the baby is fully grown.

My mom will carry me on her back until I'm about three months old. When I was born, my scales were soft, but they hardened up after a couple of days.

A pangolin's long snout helps

Safe inside

Pangolins move slowly. When they sense danger, they roll into a ball with hard, sharp scales on the outside. If a baby is threatened, its mom tucks it under her tummy, then rolls herself around it.

it find yummy insects to eat.

hop to it!

Rockhopper penguins live in Antarctica, near the South Pole. Penguins are birds, but they can't fly—rockhoppers are good at jumping over stones though, which is how they got their name.

Rockhopper moms usually lay two eggs, and the parents take turns sitting on them. For the first few weeks after the babies (chicks) hatch, Mom goes for food, while Dad stands guard.

I'll stay with Mom and Dad until I'm about two months old and my baby feathers have disappeared. Then I'll be ready to take to the water.

All together now

Rockhoppers raise their families in a huge colony. All the babies stay together so they're warm and safe. Parents know their own chicks' calls, so they can find them.

Adult rockhoppers have bright head feathers that look like bushy eyebrows. Babies are covered with fluffy gray down.

Glossary

When you're learning about animal babies, it helps to know some special words. Here are the meanings of some words you'll find in this book.

algae tiny, simple forms of life that live in water.

burrow a hole or a collection of underground tunnels where animals live.

camouflage special color or markings that blend with the surroundings so an animal is hard to see.

colony a large group of animals that lives together.

down the soft, short, fluffy feathers on a baby bird, or on the chest of an adult. Down keeps the bird warm.

grooming when an animal cleans its fur or another animal's fur.

hatching when a baby animal breaks out of the egg it has grown in.

herd a group of animals that travels together.

instinct a natural feeling animals have from birth (rather than something they learn) that helps them to survive.

mammal an animal with fur that drinks its mother's milk when it's a baby.

mating when a male and female come together to produce babies.

prey an animal that's hunted for food.

tentacle one of the long, thin arms on some sea creatures, such as sea anemones and squid.

tick a tiny spiderlike creature that lives in animal fur.

How many new animals

Bye, bye! I hope you enjoyed making all these new friends. Please come back and see us soon.

Picture credits

The publisher would like to thank the following for their kind permission to reproduce their photographs:

(Key: a-above; b-below/bottom; c-center; l-left; r-right; t-top)

Alamy Images: Alaska Stock LLC 44cr; Blickwinkel 51t; Steve Bloom 6-7, 60-61; Mike Briner 17b; Rob Crandall 12cl; James Handfield-Jones 4-5; Martin Harvey 54tl; Louise Heusinkveld 24cl; Images of Africa Photobank/David Keith Jones 26-27; Niebrugge Images 53bl; Ron Niebrugge 45; Martin Smart 20-21; Jay Sturdevant 5bl; Chris Wallace 44l; **Ardea:** Thomas Dressler 57t; Tom & Pat Leeson 21t; Tom Watson 9b; **Corbis:** Walter Bieri/EPA 38-39; Daniel J. Cox 29b; Tim Davis 46-47t; DLILLC 11t, 19tr; Frank Lukasseck 24-25, 25t; Frans Lanting 2-3, 6b, 7t, 32l, 32-33; Renee Lynn 36cl; Roy Morsch 16-17; Robert Pickett 52-53; Jenny E. Ross 1; Kevin Schafer 7br; Steven Kazlowski/Science Faction 34t; Frank Siteman/Science Faction 41b; Paul Souders 56-57; Karen Su 61b; Winifred Wisiewski 10-11; **FLPA:** Fred Bavendam 55t; Tui De Roy 39br; Frans Lanting 61t; Cyril Ruoso/Minden Pictures 5r; FLIP Nicklin/Minden PIctures 15; Gerry Ellis / Minden Pictures 31t; Michael Quinton/Minden Pictures 21b; Michio Hoshino/Minden Pictures 34b; Minden Pictures/Vincent Grafhorst 57b; Chris Newbert / Minden Pictures 55cr; Chris Newbert/Minden Pictures 54-54; ZSSD/Minden Pictures 42bl; **Getty Images:** Karine Aigner 23b; K & K Ammann 48-49; Daryl Balfour 59t; Tom Brakefield 36b; Flickr/Ineke Kamps 47b; Jeff Foott 41t, 53t; Gallo Images/Heinrich van den Berg 22-23; Daisy Gilardini 28-29; Martin Harvey 10bl; Johnny Johnson 40; JV Images 37; Thomas Kitchin & Victoria Hurst 63; Peter Lilja 19tl; Peter Lillie 23t, 42-43; C. S. Ling 18-19; Michael Orton 34-35; PHOTO 24 25cr; Michael S. Quinton 50cl; Roy Toft 13b; Federico Veronesi 11b; **naturepl.com:** Mark Carwardine 14; Gertrud & Helmut Denzau 33tr; Anup Shah 8-9, 9t, 31b; **NHPA/Photoshot:** Dave Watts 30-31; **Jari Peltomäki:** 50-51; **Photolibrary:** Doug Lindstrand 53br; OSF/Werner Bollmann 12-13t; Picture Press 29t; **Reuters:** 58-59; **Still Pictures:** Robert Villani 12b

Jacket images: Front: Corbis: Paul Souders l; **Getty Images:** Fotofeeling tr; **NHPA/Photoshot:** David Chapman br; Andy Rouse cr; Kevin Schafer crb. **Back: Corbis:** Frank Lukasseck tr; **Getty Images:** Gandee Vasan l. **Spine: Corbis:** Paul Souders t; **Getty Images:** Fotofeeling ca; **NHPA/Photoshot:** David Chapman b; Andy Rouse c; Kevin Schafer cb

All other images © Dorling Kindersley
For further information see: www.dkimages.com

have you discovered?

Index

Dorling Kindersley would like
to thank Wendy Horobin,
Deborah Lock, and Alexander
Cox for editorial help.